EAST LONDON LINE

Vic Mitchell and Keith Smith

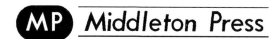
MP Middleton Press

Cover picture: Ex-LNER nos 68646 and 68633 proceed towards New Cross Gate with a football special from Norwich on 2nd November 1957. It has run through the Thames Tunnel and has just passed over Surrey Canal Junction. (J.J.Smith)

Published August 1996

ISBN 1 873793 80 4

Design - Deborah Goodridge

Published by Middleton Press
            Easebourne Lane
            Midhurst
            West Sussex
            GU29 9AZ
            Tel: 01730 813169
            Fax: 01730 812601

Printed & bound by Biddles Ltd,
            Guildford and Kings Lynn

CONTENTS

77	Canada Water
7	Electric Stock
1	Locomotives
116	Liverpool Street
58	New Cross
15	New Cross Gate
79	Rotherhithe
92	Shadwell
105	Shoreditch
95	St. Mary's
68	Surrey Quays
84	Wapping
96	Whitechapel

ACKNOWLEDGEMENTS

We are very grateful for assistance received from those mentioned in the photographic credits and also for help given by D.Catling, G.Croughton, D.Cullum, P.Hay, R.Humphries (LUL), N.Langridge, D.Monk-Steel, G.Patterson (LUL), Mr.D. and Dr.S. Salter, G.T.V.Stacey, M.J.Streatton and our ever supportive wives.

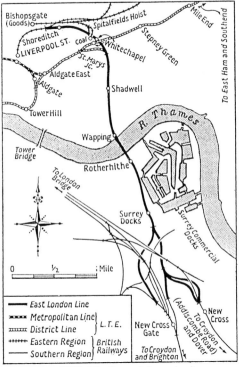

1953 (Railway Magazine)

GEOGRAPHICAL SETTING

South of Shadwell the 5½ mile long route was constructed on or in the mud and silts of the Alluvium of the Thames Valley, east of the boundaries of the City of London. North of Shadwell, the line is in Flood Plain Gravels.

All maps are to the scale of 25 ins to 1 mile, unless otherwise shown.

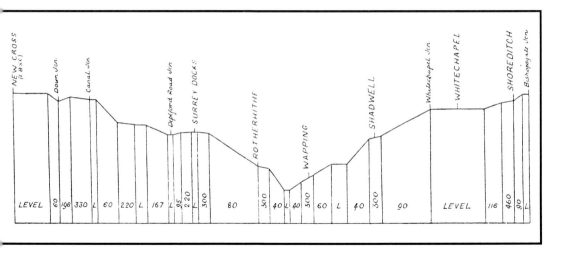

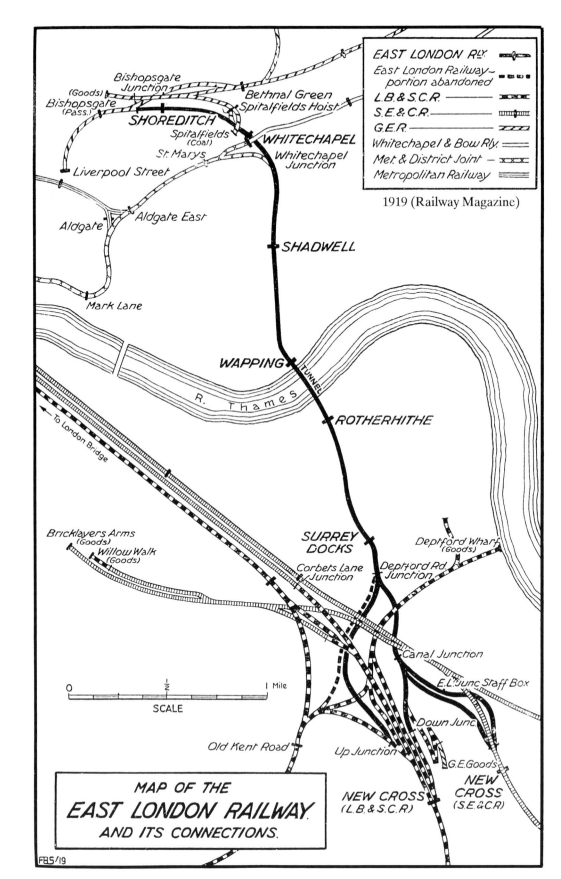

Legend (1919 Railway Magazine):
- EAST LONDON RLY.
- East London Railway — portion abandoned
- L.B.&S.C.R.
- S.E.&C.R.
- G.E.R.
- Whitechapel & Bow Rly.
- Met. & District Joint
- Metropolitan Railway

1919 (Railway Magazine)

Bishopsgate Junction
Bishopsgate (Goods)
Bishopsgate (Pass.)
SHOREDITCH
Bethnal Green
Spitalfields Hoist
Spitalfields (Coal)
St. Marys
WHITECHAPEL
Whitechapel Junction
Liverpool Street
Aldgate East
Aldgate
Mark Lane
SHADWELL
R. Thames
WAPPING TUNNEL
ROTHERHITHE
To London Bridge
Bricklayers Arms (Goods)
Willow Walk (Goods)
SURREY DOCKS
Deptford Wharf (Goods)
Corbets Lane Junction
Deptford Rd Junction
Canal Junction
E.L. Junc Staff Box
Down Junc.
Old Kent Road
Up Junction
G.E. Goods
NEW CROSS (L.B.&S.C.R.)
NEW CROSS (S.E.&C.R.)

0   ½   1 Mile
SCALE

MAP OF THE
EAST LONDON RAILWAY
AND ITS CONNECTIONS.

FBS/19

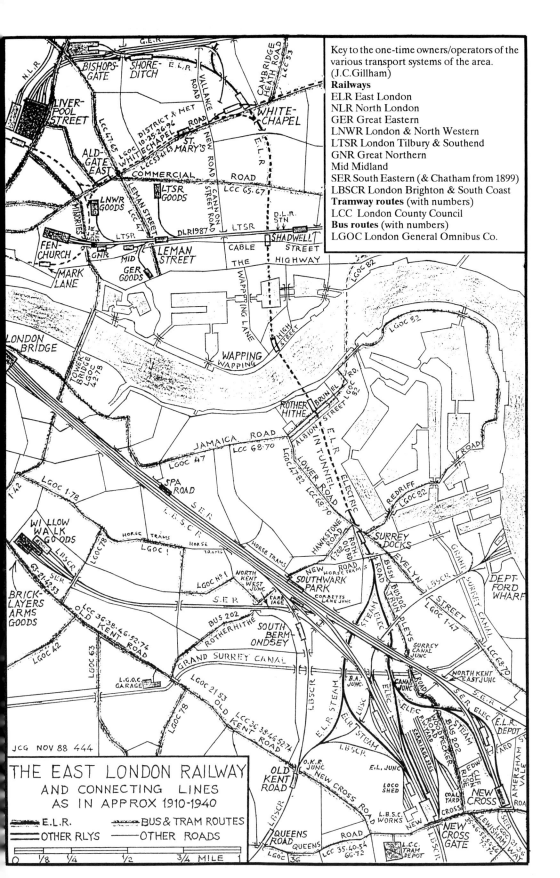

Key to the one-time owners/operators of the various transport systems of the area.
(J.C.Gillham)
Railways
ELR East London
NLR North London
GER Great Eastern
LNWR London & North Western
LTSR London Tilbury & Southend
GNR Great Northern
Mid Midland
SER South Eastern (& Chatham from 1899)
LBSCR London Brighton & South Coast
Tramway routes (with numbers)
LCC London County Council
Bus routes (with numbers)
LGOC London General Omnibus Co.

THE EAST LONDON RAILWAY
AND CONNECTING LINES
AS IN APPROX 1910-1940

JCG NOV 88 444

- E.L.R.
- OTHER RLYS
- BUS & TRAM ROUTES
- OTHER ROADS

0   1/8   1/4   1/2   3/4 MILE   1

HISTORICAL BACKGROUND

Southern developments

The London & Greenwich Railway was the first line in the area, the principal part of it opening in 1836. It became part of the SER in 1845 and a branch south from it (to Dartford and beyond via Lewisham) in 1849 resulted in a station being provided at New Cross.

The London & Croydon Railway opened on 5th June 1839 and shared the LGR route at its London end. New Cross gained its first station on that date, this receiving the suffix "Gate" in 1923. The line became part of the LBSCR in 1846. This company opened the first part of its South London Line on 13th August 1866 and built stations at Old Kent Road and Peckham Rye at which ELR trains would eventually terminate.

Northern developments

The Eastern Counties Railway reached its first London terminus at Shoreditch on 1st July 1840, the station being renamed Bishopsgate in 1846. The ECR became part of the GER in 1862 and the line was extended to Liverpool Street on 2nd February 1874 for suburban traffic, other passenger trains following on 1st November 1875.

The London & Blackwall Railway and its successor, the LTSR, had no physical rail link with the ELR and therefore are not considered here.

The Metropolitan and District Railways' joint scheme for completion of the Inner Circle and the provision of a branch towards Whitechapel was slow to be fulfilled. This station did not open until 6th October 1884 and was District Railway property.

The Thames Tunnel

The Thames Tunnel Company received its Act of Parliament on 24th June 1824 and digging commenced in Rotherhithe on 25th November 1825, under the supervision of Marc Brunel. A development of his patented tunnelling shield was the key to success, refinements of the system subsequently being used in all soft-ground tunnels. Despite the use of this device, the river broke in and flooded the workings five times. In places, there was only 14ft of mud between the crown of the tunnel and the bed of the river.

The engineer's now more famous son, Isambard Kingdom Brunel, was appointed resident engineer in 1827. His father subsequently suffered ill health, the company had chronic financial difficulties, the miners were prone to strike, the methane caused fires, the foul water and air gave rise to severe disabilities, Isambard suffered leg injuries while escaping one of the sudden floods and work stopped for five years. However, the 1200ft long tunnel reached the Wapping shaft in November 1841 and it was opened to pedestrians in March 1843.

Funds were not forthcoming for the construction of the proposed spiral approach roads and so the project was a financial disaster and did little to relieve the chronic traffic congestion on London Bridge. It housed market stalls during the day and "undesirables" at night. Having been built large enough to accommodate loaded hay carts, the tunnel was to have a second use as the railway era developed.

East London Railway and later

The ELR Company acquired the Thames Tunnel in September 1865 and a passenger service commenced between New Cross (LBSCR) and Wapping on 7th December 1869. It was operated by the LBSCR and services to that company's Old Kent Road station started on 13th March 1871. A single line up spur from their New Cross station to Deptford Road junction was opened on 1st July 1876.

Extension northward involved destruction of property and difficult tunnelling under London Docks, but trains ran through to Liverpool Street from 10th April 1876, all being worked by the LBSCR. ELR trains ran to New Cross (SER) from 1st April 1880.

A connection between the ELR and the Metropolitan & District Joint Line west of Whitechapel (at St. Mary's) came into use on 3rd March 1884, but a tunnel for an eastward spur to the GER at Cambridge Heath was never completed.

An agreement of 1882 allowed control of the company by a joint committee of lessees. It comprised the Metropolitan, Metropolitan District, GER (from 1885), SER, LCDR and LBSCR. The last was responsible for maintenance until 1885 when the SER took over. The Company was in receivership from

1878 until 1889 and never ran a train of its own.

Electric trains using the four rail system commenced between both New Cross stations and Shoreditch on 31st March 1913. Power was supplied by the District Railway, conductor rails and trains were provided by the Metropolitan and civil engineering and track relaying was undertaken by the SECR. The GER continued to work most of the goods traffic, this having started in about 1880. The LNER assumed responsibility for this in 1923.

The ELR was transferred to the Southern Railway under a 1925 Act but it was still managed by a joint committee. The Metropolitan and District interests were taken over by the London Passenger Transport Board in 1933, which became responsible for the line's passenger services. The route carried heavy military traffic in both World Wars.

Joint control ceased upon nationalisation in 1948 when the London Transport Executive became solely in charge of the route. However, freight services were operated over the line by the Eastern Region of British Railways.

Closure

The route closed to regular goods traffic in 1962 but occasional parcels trains ran until 16th April 1966.

Complete closure took place on 25th March 1995 for what was intended to be a period of seven months. This was to allow the construction of a new station at Canada Water, waterproofing of the tunnel and resignalling. A few hours prior to work starting on the tunnel, it was listed Grade II*. Complex negotiations between various organisations were protracted and included threat of permanent closure. Compromise was eventually reached but at the expense of loss of traffic over a long period (during which this book was compiled). Reopening in 1997 was anticipated.

The future

London Underground Ltd published proposals in 1993 to extend the ELL north and south to, at last, realise the potential of the route, using Private Finance Initiative.

Plans included closure of Shoreditch station and the construction of a new section of track from that point, over the ex-GER main line, through the disused Bishopsgate Goods Depot (where a station would be built) and on to the disused trackbed between Broad Street and Dalston Junction. Stations would be provided at the latter place and at Hoxton and Haggerston. Highbury might be the northern terminus for trains.

Reopening of former BR connections could give southern destinations such as East Croydon, West Croydon, Clapham Junction and Wimbledon, all depending upon Railtrack access.

PASSENGER SERVICES

Services were provided to both New Cross stations in approximately equal numbers from 1913. To list the varying train frequencies would be tedious and so we show below the interesting changes of destinations of ELL trains.

1869 (7 December) New Cross (LBSCR)-Wapping started (LBSCR)
1871 (13 March) Old Kent Road-Wapping started (LBSCR)
1876 (10 April) New Croydon-Liverpool St. started (LBSCR) Old Kent Road - Shoreditch started (LBSCR)
1876 (1 November) Brighton-Liverpool St. started (LBSCR)
1877 (1 August) Old Kent Road services extended to Peckham Rye
1880 (1 April) Addiscombe Road-Liverpool Street services started (SER)
1881 (1 November) Crystal Palace-Liverpool Street services started (LBSCR)
1882 (30 August) Crystal Palace services ceased
1883 (1 October) Brighton services ceased
1884 (3 March) SER trains operated to St.Mary's temporary terminus until 30 September
1884 (1 October) MDR Hammersmith to New Cross (LBSCR station) via Mansion House and MR

Hammersmith to New Cross (SER station) via Kings Cross services started. SER trains withdrawn.
1886 (1 January) GER trains operate Liverpool St. services and LBSCR trains terminate at Shoreditch or Whitechapel.
1886 (1 January) LBSCR Croydon services ceased
1887 (1 February) GER trains to New Croydon started, some running to Central Croydon until 1890.
1905 (1 August) MDR trains ceased following electrification of its main route. Replaced by more LBSCR trains to Shoreditch and a few SECR peak hour services to Whitechapel.
1906 (2 December) MR trains ceased following electrification of its main route.
1911 (30 June) All journeys south of New Cross ceased, also those to Peckham Rye.
1913 (31 March) Electric services from Kensington Addison Road via Kings Cross started and electric trains commenced between New Cross and Shoreditch, operated by the MR. Liverpool Street trains ceased.
1914 (9 February) MR trains started at Hammersmith instead of Kensington Addison Road.
1936 (4 May) Hammersmith services in peak hours only, also Whitechapel-Shoreditch.
1941 (6 October) Hammersmith services withdrawn.

CROYDON, BECKENHAM, NEW CROSS, and LIVERPOOL STREET.— S.E. [Sundays.

	mrn	mrn	mrn	mrn	mrn	mrn	aft	aft	aft	aft	aft	aft	aft	aft	aft	mrn	mrn	aft	aft	aft	aft	aft
Croydn(Addiscombe) d																						
Woodside																						
Elmer's End																						
New Beckenham																						
Lower Sydenham																						
Catford Bridge																						
Lady Well																						
St. John's																						
New Cross (S. E.)																						
Deptford Road																						
Rotherhithe																						
Wapping																						
Shadwell																						
Whitechapel																						
Shoreditch																						
Liverpool Street..arr																						

August 1881

EAST LONDON LINE and the CRYSTAL PALACE.—L. B. & S. C.

	mrn	mrn	aft	aft	aft	aft	aft	aft	aft			mrn	mrn	aft	aft	aft	aft	aft	aft	aft
Liverpool Street d										Crystal Palace dep										
Shoreditch										Gipsy Hill										
Whitechapel										Lower Norwood										
Shadwell										Tulse Hill										
Wapping										North Dulwich										
Rotherhithe										Champion Hill										
New Cross										Peckham Rye										
Brockley										Queen's Road										
Forest Hill										Old Kent Road										
Sydenham										Sydenham										
Old Kent Road										Forest Hill										
Queen's Road										Brockley										
Peckham Rye										New Cross										
Champion Hill										Deptford Road										
North Dulwich										Rotherhithe										
Tulse Hill										Wapping										
Lower Norwood										Shadwell										
Gipsy Hill										Whitechapel										
Crystal Palace arr										Shoreditch										
										Liverpool Street a										

July 1882

EAST LONDON.

Shoreditch to Peckham Rye at 5 22, 6 20, 7 26, 8 29, 9, 9 59, 10 20, 11 9, and 11 30 mrn.; 12 15, 1 19, 3 3, 4 15, 5 38, 6 49, 8 3, 9 4, and 10 13 aft. SUNDAYS at 9 20 and 10 28 mrn.; 1 18, 2 50, 3 41, 4 48, 4 50, 6 20, 6 40, 7 30, 8 30, and 10 20 aft. **Peckham Rye to Shoreditch** at 5 53, 6 55, 7 59, 8 59, 9 28, 10 35, 10 50, and 11 40 mrn.; 12 50, 1 24, 2 29, 3 33, 5 10, 6 14, 7 22, 8 37, 9 33, and 10 50 aft. SUNDAYS at 9 55 and 10 55 mrn.; 1 50, 3 34, 4 20, 4 44, 5 42, 6 49, 7 20, 8 9, and 10 50 aft. The Trains call at Whitechapel 2, Shadwell 5, Wapping 7, Rotherhithe 9, Deptford Road 12, Old Kent Road 16, Queen's Road 18, arriving at Peckham Rye 20 minutes after leaving Shoreditch.

Shoreditch to New Cross (L. B. & S. C.) at 5 18, 5 40, 6 13, 6 54, 7 33, 7 55, 8 42, 9 30, 9 43, 10 33, and 11 33 mrn.; 12, 1 3, 1 37, 2 2, 2 55, 3 29, 3 56, 4 32, 4 55, 5 30, 5 55, 6 34, 7 49, 8 23, 8 49, 9 28, 10 44, and 11 29 aft. SUNDAYS at 8 24, 9 24, 9 44, 10 23, 10 44, 11 25, and 11 40 mrn.; 12 45, 12 58, 1 50, 2 14, 2 29, 3 29, 4 43, 5 21, 6 13, 7 21, 7 53, 8 22, 8 52, 9 30, 9 53, 11 8, and 11 23 aft. **New Cross (L. B. & S. C.) to Shoreditch** at 4 59, 5 15, 5 43, 6 13, 7 15, 8 16, 8 25, 9 17, 9 55, 10 5, 11 4, and 11 18 mrn.; 12 24, 1 5, 2 27, 2 47, 3 26, 4 5, 4 20, 5 56, 7 20, 7 55, 8 16, 8 55, 9 47, and 10 15 aft. SUNDAYS at 7 47, 8 45, 9 14, 9 49, 10 15, 10 45, and 11 15 mrn.; 12 22, 12 43, 1 8, 1 25, 2 14, 2 48, 3 14, 4 15, 5 25, 6 3, 6 37, 7 48, 8 15, 9 19, 9 55, 10 25, and 10 40 aft. Trains call at Whitechapel 2, Shadwell 5, Wapping 7, Rotherhithe 9, Deptford Road 12, arriving at New Cross 16 minutes after leaving Shoreditch.

Liverpool Street (Great Eastern) to New Cross (L. B. & S. C.) at 5 15, 6 10, 7 30, 8 39, 9 40, 10 30, 11 30, and 11 57 mrn.; 1, 1 34, 2 52, 3 53, 4 29, 5 27, 6 31, 7 46, and 8 46 aft. SUNDAYS at 9 21 and 10 20 mrn.; 12 55, 2 13, 3 26, 4 40, 6 10, 7 18, 8 19, and 9 50 aft. **New Cross (L. B. & S. C.) to Liverpool Street** at 5 43, 8 16, 9 17, 10 5, 11 4, and 11 18 mrn.; 12 24, 1 5, 2 27, 3 26, 4 5, 5, 5 56, 7 20, 8 16, 9 15, and 9 47 aft. SUNDAYS at 9 49 and 10 45 mrn.; 1 25, 2 48, 4 15, 5 25, 6 37, 7 48, 9 19, and 10 25 aft. The Trains call at Shoreditch 3, Whitechapel 5, Shadwell 8, Wapping 10, Rotherhithe 12, Deptford Road 15, arriving at New Cross 19 minutes after leaving Liverpool Street.

St. Mary's to New Cross (South Eastern) at 6, 6 17, 6 47, 7 17, 7 47, 8 7, 8 27, 8 48, 9 7, 9 27, 9 48, 10 7, 10 27, 10 47, 11 7, 11 27, and 11 47 mrn.; 12 7, 12 27, 12 47, 1 7, 1 27, 1 47, 2 7, 2 27, 2 47, 3 7, 3 27, 3 48, 4 7, 4 27, 4 48, 5 7, 5 27, 5 48, 6 7, 6 27, 6 48, 7 7, 7 27, 7 48, 8 7, 8 27, 8 47, 9 17, 9 47, 10 17, and 11 47 aft. SUNDAYS at 8 48, 9 18, 9 48, 10 18, 10 48, and 11 8 mrn.; and every half-hour from 1 48 to 10 48, and 11 28 aft. **New Cross (South Eastern) to St. Mary's** at 5 51, 6 1, 6 21, 6 29, 6 51, 7 11, 7 21, every 20 minutes from 7 51 mrn. to 8 51, and at 9 51, 10 21, 10 51, and 11 21 aft. SUNDAYS at 7 51, 8 21, 8 51, 9 21, 9 51, and 10 21 mrn.; every half-hour from 12 51 to 10 21 aft. Trains call at Shadwell 4, Wapping 6, Deptford Road 11, arriving at New Cross 15 minutes after leaving St. Mary's.

St. Mary's to New Cross (L. B. & S. C.) at 6 11 and every half-hour from 6 42 mrn. to 9 42 aft., and at 10 7, 10 42, 11 5, 11 42, and 12 7 night. SUNDAYS at 8 12, 8 37, 9 12, 9 42, 9 54, 10 12, 10 42, 10 54, and 11 24 mrn.; and every half-hour from 1 35 to 11 5 aft. **New Cross (L. B. & S. C.) to St. Mary's** every half-hour from 6 8 mrn. to 9 8, 9 34, 10 8, 10 38, 11 8, and 11 34 aft. SUNDAYS at 8 8, 8 38, 9 8, 9 38, 10 8, 10 19, and 10 38 mrn.; and every half-hour from 12 28 to 10 58 aft. The Trains call at Shadwell 4, Wapping 6, Rotherhithe 8, Deptford Road 11, arriving at New Cross 15 minutes after leaving St. Mary's.

February 1887

LIVERPOOL STREET, NEW CROSS, and PECKHAM RYE.—East London.

Secretary and Manager, W. H. Parsons, 31, Queen Street, E.C.

	Week Days.							Sundays.						
	First			Last				First				Last		
	mrn	mrn	mrn	aft	aft	aft	ngt.	mrn	mrn	mrn	mrn	aft	aft	aft	aft
Liverpool Street..........dep.	5 2	....	....		9 58					8 40		9 50			
Shoreditch....................	5 8	5 22	....	10	1 10	10	....12 7		8 24	8 43	9 10	9 53	10 21	....11 51	
Whitechapel..................	5 10	5 24	6 12	10	3 10	12 11	5 42 12 9	8 0	8 26	8 45	9 12	9 55	10 23	11 38	11 53
Shadwell and St. George's East......	5 13	5 27	6 15	10	6 10	15 11	57 12 12	8 3	8 29	8 48	9 15	9 58	10 26	11 41	11 56
Wapping........................	5 15	5 29	6 17	10	8 10	17 11	59 12 14	8 5	8 31	8 50	9 17	10 0	10 28	11 43	11 58
Rotherhithe....................	5 17	5 31	6 19	10	10 10	19 12	1 12 16	8 7	8 33	8 52	9 19	10 2	10 30	11 45	12 0
Deptford Road for Southwark Park..	5 20	5 34	6 22	10	13 10	22 12	4 12 19	8 10	8 36	8 55	9 22	10 5	10 33	11 48	12 3
New Cross (L. B. & S. C.)........arr.	5 24	....	....	10	17	....	....12 23	8 40	8 59	....	10 9	....	....	12 7	
" (S. E. & C.)........ "	....	....	6 26	....		12 8	12 8	8 14	....	....		....	11 52	....	
Old Kent Road................	....	5 38	....	10	26	....			....	....	9 26		10 37	....	
Queen's Road..................	....	5 40	....	10	28	....			....	....	9 28		10 39	....	
Peckham Rye..............arr.	....	5 42	....	10	30	....			....	....	9 30		10 41	....	

	Week Days.							Sundays.						
	First			Last				First				Last		
	mrn	mrn	mrn	mrn	aft	aft	aft	aft	mrn	mrn	mrn	mrn	aft	aft	aft	aft
Peckham Rye................dep.	....	....	....		10 50					9 55		10 54			
Queen's Road....................	....	....	....	6 0	10 53					9 58		10 57			
Old Kent Road..................	....	....	....	6 2	10 55					10 0		10 59			
New Cross (S. E. & C.).......dep.	....	....	5 51		11 34				7 40	....		11 20			
" (L. B. & S. C.) "	4 45	5 30	....	10 47	....11 42		7 47	9 26	....10 47	11 16			
Deptford Road, for Southwark Park..	4 49	5 34	5 55	6 6	10 51	10 59	11 38	11 46	7 45	7 51	9 30	10	4 10	53 11 3	11 20 11 25
Rotherhithe....................	4 51	5 36	5 57	6 8	10 53	11 1	11 40	11 48	7 47	7 53	9 32	10	6 10	55 11 5	11 22 11 27
Wapping........................	4 53	5 38	5 59	6 10	10 55	11 3	11 42	11 50	7 49	7 55	9 34	10	8 10	55 11 7	11 24 11 29
Shadwell and St. George's East......	4 56	5 41	6 2	6 13	10 58	11 6	11 45	11 53	7 52	7 58	9 37	10	11 10	58 11 10	11 27 11 32
Whitechapel....................	4 59	5 44	6 5	6 16	11 1	11 9	11 48	11 56	7 55	8 1	9 40	10	14 11	1 11 13	11 30 11 35
Shoreditch....................	5 1	5 47	....	6 18	11 4	11 11	....11 58		8 3	9 42	10	16 11	1 11 15	11 32	....
Liverpool Street..........arr.	....	5 50	....	6 20		11 7				9 45		11 7			

Liverpool Street to New Cross (L. B. & S. C.) at 5 2, 5 55, 7 7, 9 47, 10 29, 11 32, and 11 57 mrn.; 12 55, 1 27, 2 53, 3 56, 5 27, 6 29, 7 53, 8 46, and 9 58 aft.

SUNDAYS at 8 40 and 10 18 mrn.; 12 47, 2 11, 3 27, 4 40, 6 10, 7 18, 8 19, and 9 50 aft.

New Cross (L. B. & S. C.) to Liverpool Street 5 30, 9 23, 10 3, 11 6, and 11 22 mrn.; 12 24, 1 2, 2 24, 3 17, 4 56, 5 56, 7 18, 8 17, 9 25, 9 55, and 10 47 aft.

SUNDAYS at 9 26 and 10 57 mrn.; 1 45, 2 48, 4 15, 5 26, 6 45, 7 43, 9 18, and 10 47 aft.

Shoreditch to Peckham Rye at 5 22, 6 24, 6 40, 7 26, 8 30, 9, 9 59, 11 6, and 11 30 (Sats. only) mrn.; 12 17, 1 23 (Sats. only), 3 4, 4 12, 5 38, 6 51, 8, 9 4, and 10 12 aft.

SUNDAYS at 9 10 and 10 25 mrn.; 1 20, 2 51, 3 41, 4 10, 4 51, 6 21, 7 30, 8 30, and 10 21 aft.

Peckham Rye to Shoreditch at 5 57, 6 20, 6 59, 7 14, 7 59, 9, 9 32, 10 41, and 11 51 mrn.; 12 54 (Sats. only), 1 25, 2 30 (Sats. only), 3 35, 5 10, 6 19, 7 22, 8 37, 9 37, and 10 50 aft.

SUNDAYS at 9 55 and 10 55 mrn.; 2 2, 3 34, 4 13, 4 43, 5 40, 6 49, 8 2, 9 2, and 10 54 aft.

Shoreditch and New Cross (L. B. & S. C.).—Trains run about every 20 minutes on Week Days and Sundays.

Whitechapel and New Cross (S. E.).—Trains run about every 20 minutes on Week Days and about every 30 minutes on Sundays.

On Sundays there are no Trains from Shoreditch to New Cross (L. B. & S. C.) between 11 36 mrn. and 12 42 noon; from New Cross (L. B. & S. C.) to Shoreditch between 11 15 mrn. and 12 21 noon; from Whitechapel to New Cross (S. E.) between 11 2 mrn. and 1 10 aft.; from New Cross (S. E.) to Whitechapel between 10 40 mrn. and 12 50 noon.

SHOREDITCH, SOUTH KENSINGTON, and NEW CROSS.—East London.

Secretary and Manager, W. H. Parsons, 31, Queen Street, E.C.

Down.	Week Days.							Sundays.							
	First				Last				First				Last		
	mrn	mrn	mrn	mrn	aft	aft	ngt.	aft	mrn	mrn	mrn	mrn	aft	aft	aft
Shoreditch	5 19	5 51	....		10 7		1212		8 6	8 24	....		1041	1126	....
Whitechapel	5 20	5 52	....		10 8		1213		8 7	8 25	....		1042	1127	....
South Kensington ...dep.	....		6 4	6 20	1120			1159		8 35	8 50	9 20			1120
Praed Street............	....		6 13	6 29	1130			1159		8 44	8 59	9 29			1129
Baker Street............	....		6 18	6 33	1134		12 3			8 48	9 3	9 33			1133
Moorgate Street........	....		6 23	6 38	1139		12 8			8 53	9 8	9 38			1138
Liverpool Street........	....		6 29	6 44	1145		1214			8 59	9 14	9 44			1144
St. Mary's..............	....		6 31	6 46	1147		1216			9 1	9 16	9 46			1146
	....		6 35	6 50	1151		1220			9 5	9 20	9 50			1150
Shadwell & St. George's East	5 22	5 54	6 37	6 52	1010	1153	1215	1222	8 9	8 27	9 7	9 22	9 52	1044	1129 1152
Wapping................	5 24	5 56	6 39	6 54	1012	1155	1217	1224	8 11	8 29	9 9	24 9	54	1046	1131 1154
Rotherhithe........[Park	5 26	5 58	6 41	6 56	1014	1157	1219	1226	8 13	8 31	9 11	9 26	9 56	1048	1133 1156
Surrey Docks, fr Southwark	5 28	6 0	6 43	6 58	1016	1159	1221	1228	8 15	8 33	9 13	9 28	9 58	1050	1135 1158
New Cross (L. B. & S.C.). arr.	5 32	....		7 3	1020	12 3	....		8 19	....		9 32	10 2	1054	....
" (S. E. & C.).. "	....		6 4	6 47	....		1225	1232	8 37	9 17	....		113912 2	

Up.	Week Days.							Sundays.							
	First				Last				First				Last		
	mrn	mrn	mrn	mrn	aft	aft	aft		mrn	mrn	mrn	mrn	aft	aft	aft
New Cross (S. E. & C.)..dep.	4 43	5 4	....		1123		1143		7 28	8 1	....		1014	....11 7	
" (L. B. & S. C.) "	....		5 13	5 34	1028		1137		7 45	....	8 38	10 8	....	11 1	
Surrey Docks, fr Southwark	4 47	5 8	5 17	5 38	1032	1127	1141	1147	7 32	7 49	8 5	8 42	1012	1018 11 5	1111
Rotherhithe........[Park	4 49	5 10	5 19	5 40	1034	1129	1143	1149	7 34	7 51	8 7	8 44	1014	1020 11 7	1113
Wapping................	4 50	5 11	5 20	5 41	1035	1130	1144	1150	7 35	7 52	8 8	8 45	1015	1021 11 8	1114
Shadwell & St. George's East	4 52	5 13	5 22	5 43	1037	1132	1146	1152	7 37	7 54	8 10	8 47	1017	1023 1110	1116
St. Mary's..............	....		5 16	5 25	....	1135	1149	....	7 40	....		8 50	1020	....	1119
Liverpool Street........	....		5 20	5 29	....	1139	1153	....	7 44	....		8 54	1024	....	1123
Moorgate Street........	....		5 21	5 30	....	1140	1154	....	7 45	....		8 55	1025	....	1124
King's Cross............	....		5 28	5 37	....	1147	12 1	....	7 58	....		9 2	1032	....	1135
Baker Street............	....		5 34	5 42	....	1152	12 6	....	8 3	....		9 7	1037	....	1140
Praed Street............	....		5 38	5 46	....	1156	1210	....	8 7	....		9 11	1041	....	1146
South Kensington....arr.	....		5 47	5 55	....	12 5	1219	....	8 17	....		9 20	1052	....	1156
Whitechapel	4 54	....		5 45	1039		1154		7 56	8 12	....		1025	1112	....
Shoreditch .... arr.	4 56	....		5 47	1041		1156		7 58	8 14	....		1027	1114	....

Shoreditch and New Cross (L. B. & S. C.).—Trains run about every 15 minutes on Week Days and 30 minutes on Sundays.

Shoreditch and New Cross (S. E. & C.).—Trains run about every 15 minutes on Week Days and 30 minutes on Sundays.

South Kensington and New Cross (L. B. & S. C.). Trains run about every 30 minutes on Week Days and Sundays.

South Kensington and New Cross (S. E. & C.).—Trains run about every 30 minutes on Week Days and Sundays.

LOCOMOTIVES

1. Designed by William Stroudley, 50 of these class A (later A1) lightweight 0-6-0Ts were built for the LBSCR suburban services between 1872 and 1880 and they became one of the most commonly used engines on the ELR. Known as "Terriers", ten still exist, this condensing example being at Bressingham Steam Museum. For the opening of the line, Mr Craven provided 2-4-0Ts nos 51 and 109. (E.R.Lacey coll.)

2. The SER provided Q class 0-4-4Ts to work on the ELR. Designed by Stirling, 118 were built between 1881 and 1897 but only a few were able to condense. Unusually, the condensing pipes discharged into the left tank only. This supplied a pump whereas the other tank fed an injector. These always require cold water. (Lens of Sutton)

3. The oval Metropolitan Railway insignia is evident on their Beyer Peacock 4-4-0T no. 26, which was built in 1868. This manufacturer built similar but smaller 2-4-0T locomotives for use on the Isle of Man. Some are still in use and continue to carry numbers on their chimneys. (Lens of Sutton)

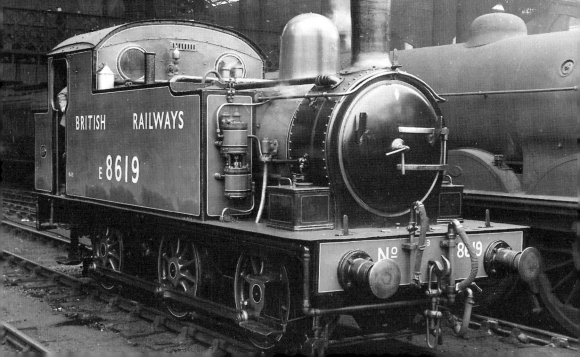

4.   The GER provided five 0-4-4Ts of class E10 for the ELR. Numbered 59, 101, 233, 586 and 588, they were built between 1879 and 1883; all were fitted with condensing equipment in 1885. The designer was Massey Bromley. (N.Bowdidge coll.)

5.   The LNER class J69 0-6-0Ts, built in 1890-1904, were employed, in later years, on most ELR freight work. This example survived to be photographed serving as Liverpool Street station pilot after nationalisation. Note that it has both air and vacuum brake pipes. (J.H. Aston)

6.   GER Holden class M15 2-4-2Ts were used on the route and carried two green discs when working from Liverpool Street to Croydon. A white light was required between Shoreditch and Deptford Road (Surrey Quays). The vans were designed to convey the carriages of the gentry. No. 101 was in use from 1905 until 1929 and was classified F4 by the LNER. (E.R.Lacey coll.)

ELECTRIC STOCK

7. Metropolitan-Cammell Ltd built a large batch of this type for the Metropolitan Railway in 1905. The photograph was taken at Hammersmith and includes one of the female guards employed in 1916-18 as a wartime measure. (Mrs E. Amos coll.)

8. The District Railway "B" stock was also constructed in 1905 and clerestory roofs were specified again. This stock was used on the route from 1937 to 1953. These coaches were probably over 50 years old when recorded at Shoreditch. Originally air controlled, the doors were converted to manual operation. (Lens of Sutton)

9. Oval end windows characterised the "F" stock which was manufactured in 1920 and used on the route between 1953 and 1963. Trains with three pairs of sliding doors per coach would not be used widely for another 50 years. (Lens of Sutton)

10. The 1923-built "G" stock was a less imaginative design with flat ends and sides, plus the traditional clerestory roof. When photographed near Surrey Docks in 1971, the stock was reclassified Q23. The ELL had this stock from 1963 until 1971. (R.Palmer)

11. The nearest vehicle in this 1971 photograph is an example of "K" stock, by that time known as Q27. Built in 1927, the cars had internal destination signs and domed ends to the roof. (R.Palmer)

12. The flared body side and stylish window ventilators typified the 1937-40 stock variously classified. "O" was designed for the Hammersmith & City service, "P" for the Metropolitan and "Q" for District routes. The differences were minor. "R" was introduced in 1949 and was of similar design, but of aluminium construction. Stock of this type was used on the route between 1971 and 1974. (R.Palmer)

13. Shortage of District Line stock resulted in the transfer of 1938 Bakerloo Line tube trains to the ELL on 13th January 1974. This specimen was recorded near Surrey Docks in August 1975. They were not used after 1977. (R.Palmer)

14. Metropolitan Line A60 stock was to be seen in the 1980s largely unpainted, this example being photographed at New Cross Gate in March 1985. This stock was introduced to the route in 1977. (F.Hornby)

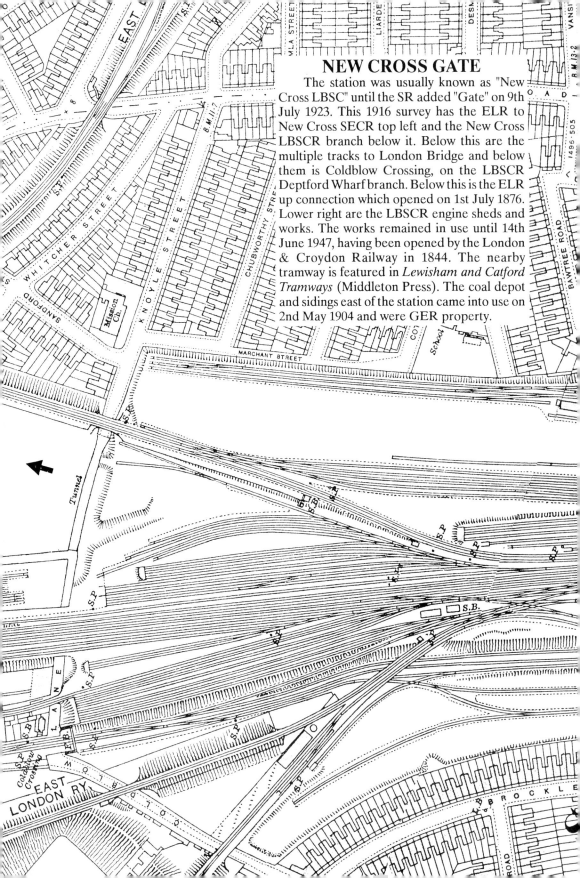

NEW CROSS GATE

The station was usually known as "New Cross LBSC" until the SR added "Gate" on 9th July 1923. This 1916 survey has the ELR to New Cross SECR top left and the New Cross LBSCR branch below it. Below this are the multiple tracks to London Bridge and below them is Coldblow Crossing, on the LBSCR Deptford Wharf branch. Below this is the ELR up connection which opened on 1st July 1876. Lower right are the LBSCR engine sheds and works. The works remained in use until 14th June 1947, having been opened by the London & Croydon Railway in 1844. The nearby tramway is featured in *Lewisham and Catford Tramways* (Middleton Press). The coal depot and sidings east of the station came into use on 2nd May 1904 and were GER property.

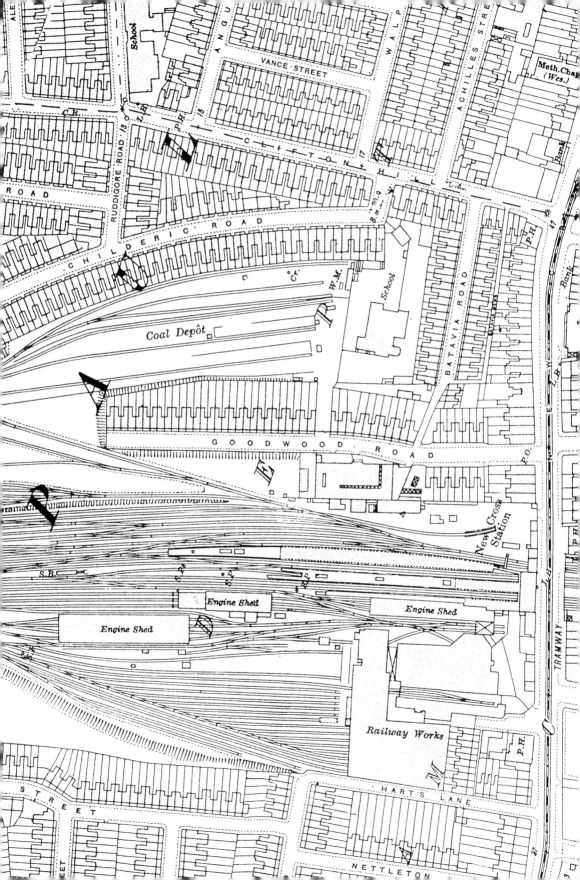

15. On the right is a tram stop and to the left of this is the list of District Railway destinations. Metropolitan trains did not serve this station for a number of years. LBSCR publicity is on the left. (Lens of Sutton)

The 1st edition of 1868 shows the ELR at the top, its independent terminus and that there was then no connection to the main line. This was added in 1877 at the same time as that to the SER. Note the two long coke ovens that produced fuel for locomotives prior to the use of coal. There are houses close to New Cross Road but otherwise the railways are adjacent to fields. It is evident that many bridges were required to give access to Coldblow Farm.

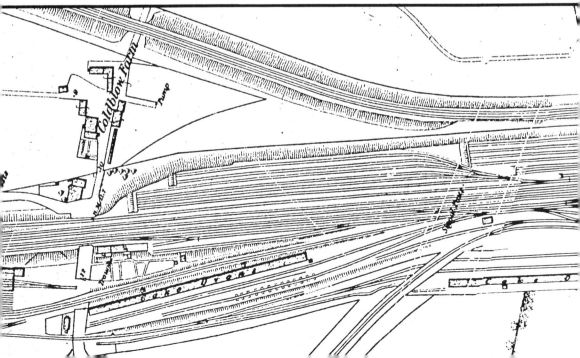

16.   Both the DR and the MR used 4-4-0Ts from Beyer Peacock & Company, all having large condensing pipes and minimum weather protection for the crews. The engines of both companies were initially painted bright olive green, but had distinctive linings. No. 22 carries the *NEW CROSS LBSC* headboard but was not photographed there. (Lens of Sutton)

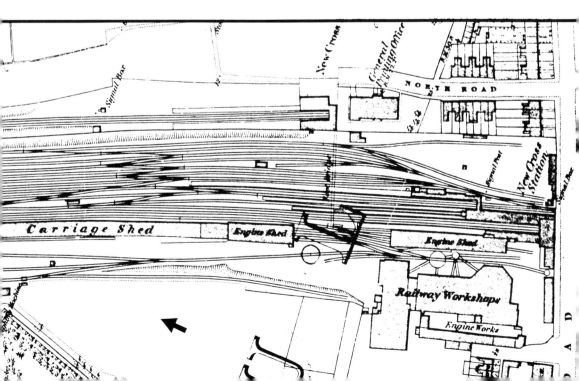

17. The destination board *NEW CROSS LBSC* is not very obvious, unlike the distinctive wishbone pipe linking the tanks. The water therein could become hot enough to release steam which was thus ducted clear of the driver's view. No. 14 was one of a batch built in 1871 by Beyer Peacock. (Lens of Sutton)

18. Standing outside one of the New Cross sheds in 1885 is "Terrier" no. 60, which was in use from 1875 until 1903. The 1887 timetable demanded that each such engine working on the ELR make 15 return trips daily. Some were named after places north of the Thames, such as *Millwall, Bishopsgate, Stepney, Shoreditch, Poplar, Wapping* and *Shadwell*. (E.R.Lacey coll.)

19. The cattle in these two wagons will no doubt have been terrified by their recent passage through the Thames Tunnel. They wait in the goods loop behind LNER class F5 2-4-2T no. 7212, which will probably be replaced by a SR engine. Most freight travelled on the ELL in the hours of darkness. (Lens of Sutton)

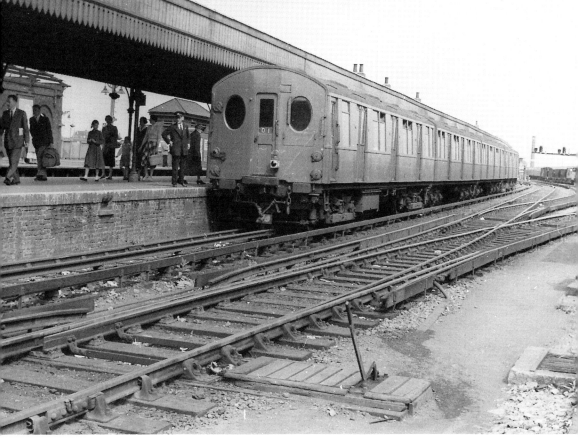

20. A return excursion from Brighton to Chingford formed of ex-GER coaches passes East London Up Junction box, which is to the right of the photographer. It is about to subject the pleasure seekers to the rigours of the Thames Tunnel with the exhaust of two hard working locomotives (nos. 68630 and 68631) on 20th June 1954. The up line to Deptford Road Junction on which this train is about to travel was closed to regular passenger trains on 1st July 1911, regular freight on 1st October 1962 and was disconnected on 1st November 1964. (S.C.Nash)

21. The "F" stock was familiar to passengers travelling north of Baker Street for many decades and it was only towards the end of its long life that some vehicles were cascaded to the ELL. The sliding doors were operated manually when built. (Lens of Sutton)

22. The "John Milton Special" ran on 3rd June 1956 and started at Crystal Palace. Change to an electric locomotive was made near New Cross Gate and it continued to Chesham via the ELL, St. Mary's curve and Baker Street. Class C2X no. 32543 is arriving with the train at platform 5. (Lens of Sutton)

23. Having left its train, no. 32543 passes an LT train of "F" stock and gives us an opportunity to see the connection between the ELL and the Southern Region down local line. (Lens of Sutton)

25. The Elsenham to Brighton excursion is entering "No. 1 Goods Arrival Road" on 21st June 1959, hauled by class 16 diesel no. D8401. The 1950 New Cross Gate Box is near the last of Gresley's fine coaches. It was in use until 20th July 1975. (J.J.Smith)

24. Another special train intended to appeal to both ramblers and railway enthusiasts was the "Essex Wealdman" which operated from Clapham Junction to Ongar on 28th September 1958. It worked via Crystal Palace (Low Level) and reversed at Liverpool Street. Ex-LNER class J69 0-6-0T no. 68577 is coupled to ex-LSWR coaches. (Unknown)

26.   A special train of horseboxes, probably from Newmarket, enters the arrival road behind ex-LNER class J69 no. 68613 on 1st September 1961. In the foreground is the complex crossover on the LT line. (S.C.Nash)

27.   LT 0-4-4T no. L44 attracted much attention when it arrived at platform 1 with a railtour on 1st October 1961. It had originated at Stanmore. The locomotive was built by the MR at Neasden to T.F.Clark's design in 1898, entering service as no. 1. It is now at the Buckinghamshire Railway Centre, carrying that number again. (R.M.Casserley)

28.   Q27, formerly "K", stock is nearest the camera on 8th July 1971. On the right is the site of the two-platform independent ELR terminus, which was in use until 1st November 1876 and again between 1st October 1884 and 1st September 1886. The station was reported demolished in about 1900, but the smaller building may have been part of it. (E.Wilmshurst)

29.   Southbound 4SUB no. 4651 makes a sharp contrast with a Shoreditch-bound tube train of 1938 vintage on 14th June 1976. The last 4SUB ran on 1st October 1983. (R.Palmer)

30.   The goods yard on the right ceased to handle public traffic on 6th November 1967 but the class 08 diesel was present on 2nd July 1977 to shunt permanent way material. The sand drag was put in place after the direct connection with BR was severed on 17th September 1972. (R.Palmer)

31.   The connection between the ELL and the BR sidings was removed on 12th January 1975. This photograph from 7th July 1977 of A60 stock arriving reveals that the sidings were used for berthing Southern Region EMUs and for track material movement. (R.Palmer)

> **Other views of this station and its associated junctions and depots are to be found in** *London Bridge to East Croydon* **in our Southern Main Lines Series. The Deptford Wharf branch is also included therein - pictures 32 to 38.**

32. A 1988 view shows the well recognised logos. With the dismemberment of BR, the rights to its emblem were conveyed to the Secretary of State for Transport in 1996. An opposition member said that he should use it as a fig leaf to cover his embarrassment over privatisation disasters. (J.Scrace)

33. The end of the ELL was rusty throughout most of 1995 and 1996 as its passengers had to travel by bus. All trace of the railway premises west of the main line were lost as Sainsburys completed a new store on the site in 1996. (M.Turvey)

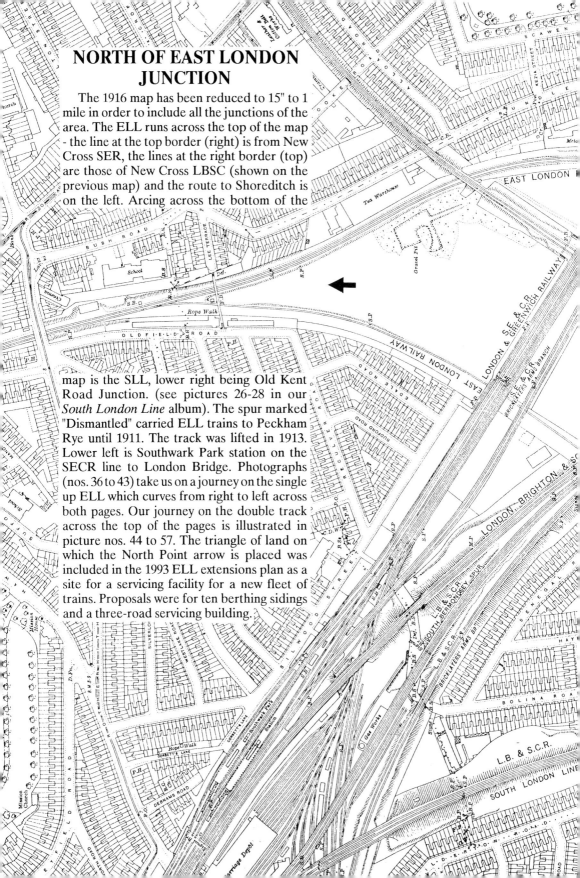

NORTH OF EAST LONDON JUNCTION

The 1916 map has been reduced to 15" to 1 mile in order to include all the junctions of the area. The ELL runs across the top of the map - the line at the top border (right) is from New Cross SER, the lines at the right border (top) are those of New Cross LBSC (shown on the previous map) and the route to Shoreditch is on the left. Arcing across the bottom of the map is the SLL, lower right being Old Kent Road Junction. (see pictures 26-28 in our *South London Line* album). The spur marked "Dismantled" carried ELL trains to Peckham Rye until 1911. The track was lifted in 1913. Lower left is Southwark Park station on the SECR line to London Bridge. Photographs (nos. 36 to 43) take us on a journey on the single up ELL which curves from right to left across both pages. Our journey on the double track across the top of the pages is illustrated in picture nos. 44 to 57. The triangle of land on which the North Point arrow is placed was included in the 1993 ELL extensions plan as a site for a servicing facility for a new fleet of trains. Proposals were for ten berthing sidings and a three-road servicing building.

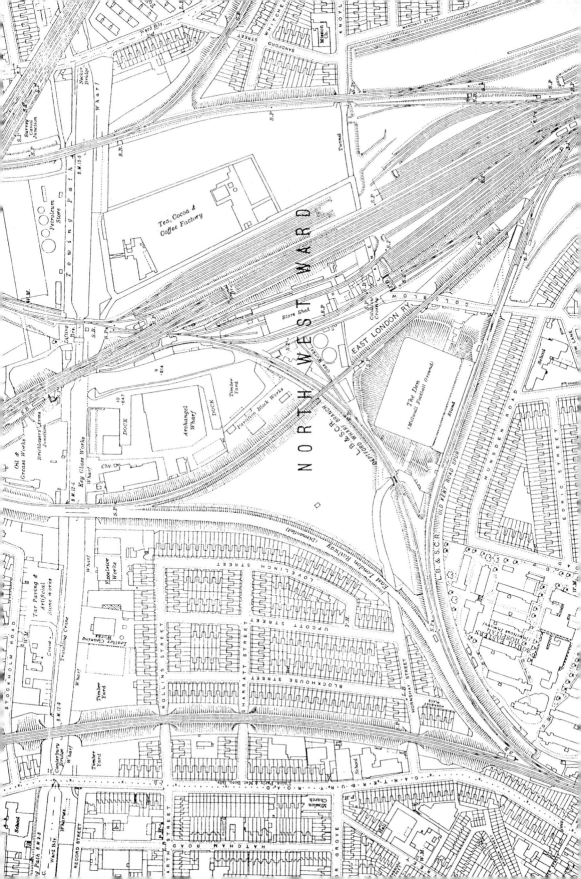

34.   A southward view from the staff footbridge over the main lines north of New Cross Gate includes the station and box of that name in the distance and East London Up Junction Box on the right. This is marked near the right border of the map and closed on 10th September 1972. LT electric locomotive no. 16 is on the left on 1st October 1961. (J.J.Smith)

35.   The Deptford Wharf branch is the non-electrified line on the left of this northward view from the same view point. The lines on the right also descend to that destination. The straight parallel quadruple track is that of the former LBSCR, to and from London Bridge. (Pamlin Prints)

36. Turning left to look west, we have the Old Kent Road Spur straight ahead and the Up ELL diverging from it on the bridge over two of the Deptford Wharf lines. Millwall Football Club's "Den" is in the background. (Pamlin Prints)

37. This eastward view was taken on 20th June 1954 from the signal seen in the previous picture. Nos. 68630 and 68631 are on the commencement of the Up ELL with a return excursion from Brighton. The signalboxes are those seen in picture no. 34 and the train was also in picture 20. (J.J.Smith)

38. A northward view of the same junction shows a train of empty stock from Eardley Sidings on the Old Kent Road Spur hauled by class 4 2-6-4T no. 42087 on 18th September 1954. The line was mainly used for this purpose until closed on 2nd November 1964. The Up ELL is on the right. (S.C.Nash)

39. The photographer is on the footbridge adjacent to Coldblow Crossing (see map) on a stormy Sunday as nos. 68630 and 68612 struggle with a return Brighton to Loughton excursion on the Up ELL. The date is 4th July 1954. (S.C.Nash)

40.   The northbound train would next pass under a bridge carrying the Bricklayers Arms branch and the main lines between New Cross Gate and London Bridge. The two spans on the left of this 1964 picture were over tracks used by Liverpool Street - Peckham Rye trains until 1911. They later spanned the access to a greyhound stadium. Bridges for the former SECR tracks are in the distance. (J.J.Smith)

41.   Now we look south under the bridges featured in the previous picture. The nearest arches were built for the London & Greenwich Railway, the first line in the district. The foot-bridge carried a public footpath but Silwood Street level crossing was for a private road. Note that the gates do not shut across the railway. (R.K.Kirkland)

42. A northward panorama from the footbridge featured in the previous illustration has Lee Terrace footbridge in the distance. The devices attached to each post gave the signalman at Canal Junction box an indication of the position of the gates. (J.J.Smith)

43. Lee Terrace was renamed Trundley's Terrace but the footbridge retained its old name. Class J69 no. 68533 reaches the end of the Up ELL as it approaches Deptford Road Junction on 26th March 1959 with the 2.17pm New Cross Gate to Temple Mills Yard. The sand was in transit from Holmethorpe (Redhill) to Harlow, where a new town was under construction. Two brake vans were provided to facilitate reversal at Liverpool Street. (J.J.Smith)

44. On the right is the point at which the ELL electrified double track becomes single to enter platform 1. No. D5095 is hauling a Stevenage to Brighton excursion on 17th May 1964. It had crossed the Thames on Blackfriars Bridge, having passed through Snow Hill Tunnel - see our *Holborn Viaduct to Lewisham* album. (J.J.Smith)

45. We now commence another journey from right to left across the last map, using the double track. A southbound train of "K" stock is passing over Knowle Street bridge (originally Knoyle), the first on our trip. There are contrasting electric and mechanical signals, one of the latter having the fish-tailed Coligny-Welch distant arm indicator. (Lens of Sutton)

46.　Passing over the same bridge is LT locomotive no. L44 with the SCTS railtour on 1st October 1961. The MR reverted to the provision of compartment stock in 1910 in response to the demands of its conservative travellers and further batches followed. (J.J.Smith)

47.　LT no. 16 *Oliver Goldsmith* was recorded a few minutes later and about 50 yds further south. It is passing the sign indicating the boundary of LT and BR maintenance responsibility. The berthing sidings are in the background of the next picture. (J.J.Smith)

48. Electric locomotive no. 16 returned with the train later that day and was recorded passing the Southern Region permanent way depot and the end of Whitcher Street. (E.Wilmshurst)

49. Minutes later another photographer pictured the special train at Canal Junction, with the New Cross line on the left. London Transport Museum houses a similar locomotive, no. 5 *John Hampden*, while no. 12 *Sarah Siddons* is in running order. (S.C.Nash)

50.   Earlier in the day, the memorable train was recorded for posterity having just passed under the former SER main line. The locomotive is on Canal Junction and the rear coach is on the canal bridge. (S.C.Nash)

51.   Taken a second or two after the previous picture, no. L44 takes the New Cross Gate route. This junction came into regular use on 1st April 1880, when the Liverpool Street - Addiscombe service commenced on the lines on the right. (E.Wilmshurst)

52. Going back in time at the same location, we witness nos. 68607 and 68549 heading for New Cross Gate where the train would termin-ate on 9th April 1955. It was carrying football supporters from Shoeburyness. (S.C.Nash)

53. Canal Junction box is evident as class J68 no. 68646 leaves the New Cross branch on 29th March 1958 with the RCTS "London Railtour" composed of a push-pull set and one 100-seat compartment coach. The train left London Bridge at 2.3pm and ran to Liverpool Street via Deptford Wharf, Bricklayers Arms and Angerstein Wharf. (J.J.Smith)

54. The east side of the ELL bridge over the Surrey Canal was photographed in 1952, having been reconstructed in 1949. The then new Bricklayers Arms Junction box is visible beyond the north abutment. The canal was infilled in 1978 to form a roadway. (R.K.Kirkland)

55. A snap from the window of the special train from Stanmore on 1st October 1961 shows the bridge carrying the former SER main line over the SLL but the adjacent footbridge is not very clear. (H.C.Casserley)

56. A Cambridge to Brighton excursion is passing under the Deptford Wharf branch on 18th July 1954, as dockland cranes adorn the skyline. The Holden locomotives, nos. 68607 and 68639, run parallel to the railwaymen's vegetable allotments. (J.J.Smith)

57. Further north we witness the two J69s accelerating the football special, seen in picture 52, away from Deptford Road Junction on 9th April 1955. In the distance is Lee Terrace footbridge seen earlier in picture no. 43. (J.J.Smith)

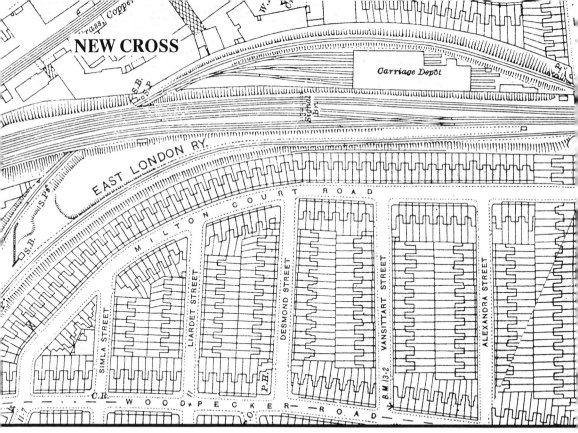

The 1916 map has the converging ELL tracks lower left and the quadruple SECR lines running across the map. A row of houses in North Kent Terrace (between Hereford Place and the station) was demolished in 1876 to make way for the ELR. The connection between the ELR and the SER was made in 1876. The first ELL trains to use the station were those on the SER service between Liverpool Street and Addiscombe, which commenced on 1st April 1880. All local passenger trains used the down single line bidirectionally from 1st October 1884. East London Junction Staff Box and its long footway is on the left. The latter was eliminated when a new box was built close to the point where the passenger line became single and a staff was required.

The October 1923 freight timetable shows most trains running at night. A footnote read "Goods Trains Working over East London Line. - All Goods Wagons must be double coupled, and no chains of any sort left hanging down. All Brake Pins must be secured in the Brake Racks and not left hanging."

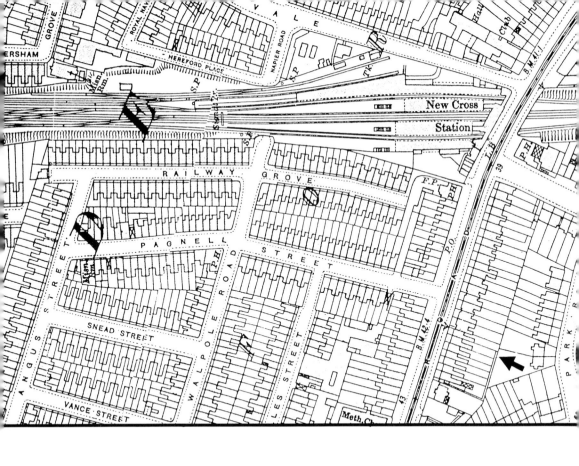

WEEK DAYS. / SUNDAYS.

From Q.E.R.	Q a.m.	Q a.m.	Q a.m.	Q a.m.	† a.m.	a.m.	Q a.m.	Q p.m.	Q p.m.	Q p.m.	Q p.m.							SUNDAYS
	NM	NM	NM	NM		NS	NS	NS	SO	N Th								
Whitechapel .... dep.	12 45	1 25	4 1	4 17	5/1	11 14	11 4	1 48	3 45	8 34	9 23	10 24	.	.	.	.	.	.
Canal Junction .... pass	12/55	1/35	4/11	4/27	5/10	11/5	11/5	1/57	3/5	8/44	9/33	10/34	.	.	.	.	.	.
New Cross .... "	1/0	1/40	4/15	4/35	5/12	11 27	11 7	1/5	3/5	8/48	9/35	10/40	.	.	.	.	.	.
St. John's .... "	1/2	1/43	4/18	4/38	5/15	11/5	11/5	2/1	3/5	8/53	9/38	10/43	.	.	.	.	.	.
Park's Bridge Junction ... "	1/10	1/45	4/20	4/38	5/17	11 12	12 1	2/	4/5	8/50	9/40	10/47	.	.	.	.	.	.
Hither Green Junction ... "	1/18	1/49	4/22	4/42	5/19	11/5	12/5	2/	4/5	9/	9/47	10/52	.	.	.	.	.	.
Hither Green Sidings ..... arr.	1 20	2 0	4 30	4 48	5 30	11 45	12 25	2 20	4 7	9 33	9 50	10 55	.	.	.	.	.	.

WEEK DAYS. / SUNDAYS.

To G.E.R.	Q a.m.	Q a.m.	Q a.m.	Q a.m.	a.m.	p.m.	Q p.m.	Q p.m.	Q p.m.	Q p.m.	Q p.m.	mdt.						SUNDAYS
	NM	NM	NM	NM			NS	NS	NS	SO	N Th	Th O	N Th					
Hither Green Sidings ...... dep	2 20	3 0	5 5	5 45	6 25	12 25	1 15	2 45	5	10 10			10 55	12 25	.	.	.	.
Hither Green Junction ...... pass	2/25	3/5	5/8	5/47	6/28	12 35	1/17	2/45	5 5	10/15			10 57	12/30	.	.	.	.
Park's Bridge Junction ...... "	2/30	3/10	5/11	5/50	6/30	12 37	1/20	2/48	5/10	10/20			11/	12/33	.	.	.	.
St. John's .... "	2/32	3/12	5/13	5/52	6/32	12 40	1 23	2 53	5/13	10/22			11/	12/37	.	.	.	.
New Cross .... "	2/35	3/15	5/15	5/54	6/35	12 43	1/25	2/55	5/15	10/25			11/ 6	12/40	.	.	.	.
Canal Junction .... "	2/37	3/17	5/17	5/56	6/38	12 46	1 27	3/	5/17	10/28	10/55		11/ 8	12/45	.	.	.	.
Whitechapel .... arr.	2 50	3 28	5 27	6 6	6 47	12 55	1 37	3 0	5 27	10 35	11 7	11 18	12 52	.	.	.	.	.

Q.—Conditional. † Starts from Spitalfields on Mondays.

58. Ex-District Railway "H" stock waits at the terminal bay as passengers alight. "H" signified hand operated doors. Prior to electrification a turntable had been sited here, which enabled engines not only to turn but to reach the run-round road. (Lens of Sutton)

59. The now familiar L44 reached New Cross on 5th September 1961 with an inspection special which is seen being propelled out of the platform. The connection from the ELL to the Southern Region down local line is included. (J.J.Smith)

60. The bridge carrying New Cross Road over the main lines also supported the station entrance and offices until 1975, when a wooden building was erected in Amersham Vale, close to the ELL platform. (J.N.Faulkner)

61. Platform 1 accommodates "K" stock on 8th July 1971 and one can see that the down local line once had two faces. Major changes in 1975 included the repositioning of the island platform and the introduction of letters A to D in place of platform numbers. (E.Wilmshurst)

62. A 1990 picture shows a longer platform canopy, the extension having taken place in 1985. "A60" stock stands at platform D, which has been linked to A and B by a subway since 1975. (T.Wright)

63. Seen from the north end of platform B, "A60" stock enters the station on 4th April 1990. The connections between the ELL and BR, on both up and down sides, were taken out of use on 16th April 1966 and removed in 1968. (F.Hornby)

64. After ten years use, the wooden building was replaced by this £5m brick built structure, which was ceremonially opened on 9th August 1985. (J.Scrace)

65.　The map shows the location of the six-road carriage shed which houses all stock for ELL services. The building was photographed through the window of a passing train in October 1990. The shed was built by the ELR and leased to the MR. (T.Wright)

66.　The non-electrified Up ELL joined the main line at Deptford Road Junction. No. L44 runs south with the railtour on 1st October 1961. A signal box had been situated to the right of the third coach. The points were disconnected on 20th February 1966. (J.Low)

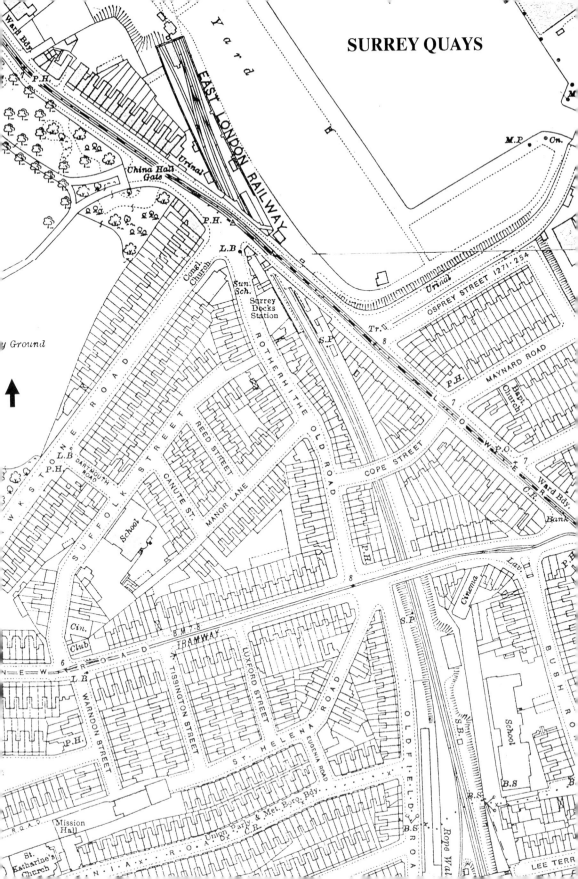

SURREY QUAYS

67. A southbound train of mixed parentage is seen from Lee Terrace footbridge on 11th September 1971, passing the site of Deptford Road Junction. The Up ELL had not been used by regular passenger trains since 1913. (R.Palmer)

The heading is on the site of Canada Dock, one of the Surrey Commercial Docks, on this 1916 edition. Near the lower border is Deptford Road Junction and the long footbridge seen in pictures 43 and 57. The single track tramway in Rotherhithe New Road had been horse worked but had ceased to be used in 1913.

68. The station was named "Deptford Road" until 17th July 1911 and "Surrey Docks" until 24th October 1989. This 1934 photograph includes the electric tramway which was opened on 26th June 1911 and which is featured in the Middleton Press *Southwark and Deptford Tramways* album. (L.T.Museum)

69. A post-war view shows the entrance which was situated between the two shops seen on the left of the previous picture. The main entrance was on the other side of the building in Rotherhithe Old Road. (H.C.Casserley coll.)

70. With snow falling, nos 68613 and 68644 pass through with an RCTS special on 29th March 1952, steam condensing widely in the cold air. The tour started at London Bridge, ran to Liverpool Street, visited many stations in suburban Essex and returned to Cannon Street via Snow Hill Tunnel.
(R.M.Casserley coll.)

71. The lengthy footway and some of the long line of columns are included in this photograph of a New Cross Gate train of "K" stock running south on 8th July 1971. (E.Wilmshurst)

72. A southward view on the same day reveals that the down platform carried another row of columns and that there had once been a bay platform adjacent. We can find no evidence that it was ever used for regular passenger traffic, although a Sunday school outing to Eastcote was reported to have used it in 1919. (E.Wilmshurst)

73. The map shows the siding arrangement that once existed between the station and the tunnel mouth on the vacant land seen in this 1971 picture. The 1923 General Instructions stated "a vehicle specially fitted for cleaning the conductor rails of snow and ice is in readiness at Surrey Docks siding. The ganger will call a steam engine from Brighton Co.'s Loco. Dept. at New Cross when required". (E.Wilmshurst)

74. Photographed on 26th August 1975 is a 1938 tube train bound for Shoreditch. Cope Street bridge is also included. Note the polite request to forgetful drivers. (R.Palmer)

75.   Plastic bags from contractor's material litter the track as work proceeds inside the illuminated tunnel during the closure period in 1996. (V.Mitchell)

76.   The station buildings were completely reconstructed between 1979 and 1982. Entrances were provided on both sides of the narrow tapering site. A Dennis accelerates round the northern apex of the station on 24th April 1996 as it works the "express" service ELX from New Cross Gate under a threatening sky. The bus operator was Walthamstow Citybus. (V.Mitchell)

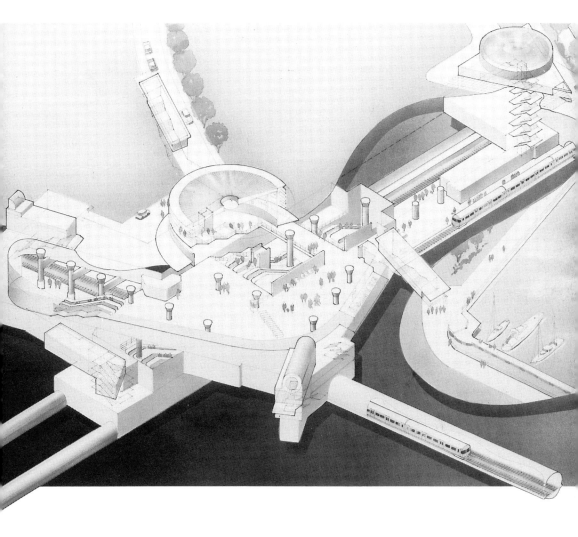

78. The ELL runs from lower right to left, while the twin tunnels of the JLE pass below, between the opposite corners. They are at a depth of 20m below ground level. (LUL)

77. A major feature of the revitalisation of the ELL was the provision of an interchange with the Jubilee Line Extension. An eastward view of progress on 9th April 1996 shows the spacious ticket hall (before roofing) and Surrey Quays Road on a temporary bridge. (LUL)

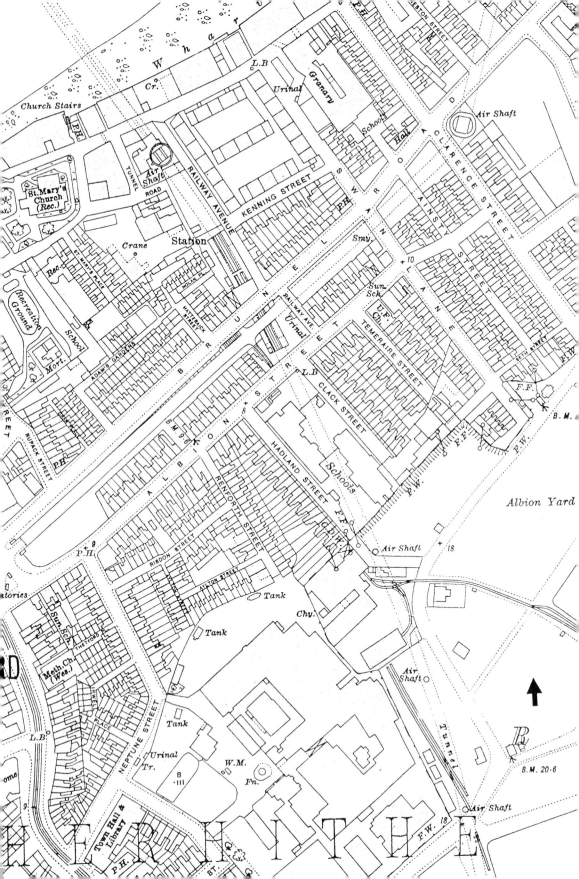

W   h   a   r   f

Church Stairs

Cr.

L.B

Urinal

Granary

D

Air Shaft

St. Mary's Church (Rec.)

Air Shaft

TUNNEL

RAILWAY ROAD

RAILWAY AVENUE

KENNING STREET

School

Hall

CLARENCE STREET

AINSTY STREET

WESTON STREET

P.H.

Crane

Station

Rec.

School

Recreation Ground

Mort.

ST. MARY'S PLACE

NOLAN PL.

MATTERICK STREET

ADAM'S GARDENS

SWAN LANE

Smy.

Sun. Sch.

U.F. Ch.

TEMERAIRE STREET

+ 10

Railway Ave

Urinal

P.H.

CLACK STREET

L.B

SEBET STREET

F.W.

F.F.

B.M.

RUPACK STREET

P.H.

B.M. 96·0

ALBION STREET

HADLAND STREET

Schools

P.H.

F.F.

F.W.

F.W.

Albion Yard

Air Shaft

+ 18

RENFORTH STREET

RISDON STREET

AVNTON STREET

THETFORD STREET

Tank

Tank

Chy.

P.H.

Air Shaft

Tunnel

tories

Sun. Sch.

Meth. Ch. (Wes.)

RWELL PLACE

NEPTUNE STREET

Tank

L.B

Urinal

Tr.

8 ·111

W.M.

Fn.

Air Shaft

P

B.M. 20·6

RD

rooms

Town Hall & Library

P.H.

ST.

E R   H   I   T   H   E

F.W.

18

Air Shaft

ROTHERHITHE

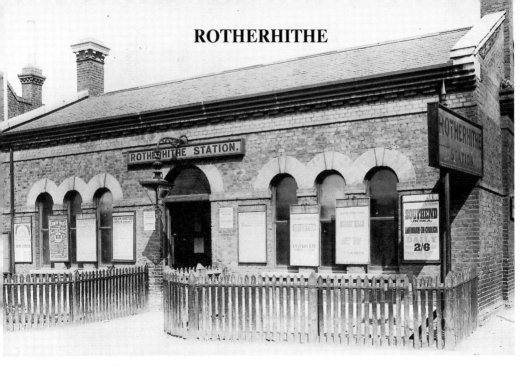

79. The first building was photographed in 1904 when one poster was offering a cheap excursion train at 10.28 on Sundays to Chalfont Rd., Chesham, Amersham, Gt. Missenden, Wendover and Aylesbury. The Seaside, Surrey Hills and Eastbourne were offered by the LBSCR as alternative sources of pleasure. (N.Bowdidge coll.)

The 1914 survey shows a number of air shafts from top to bottom, these indicating the route of the ELL. The air shaft top right is the first on the road tunnel, which opened in 1908. The access road passes over the platforms and goes underground nearby.

80. A six-foot extension was added to the old building to bring the frontage in line with other nearby premises. The work was undertaken in 1905-06 and was photographed in 1956. The join is evident. (H.C.Casserley coll.)

81. In this later view of the southbound platform we have a glimpse of the approach to the Brunels' Thames Tunnel. Behind the camera the Rotherhithe Tunnel road bridge girders intrude into the space above the platforms, as evident in the next picture. (Lens of Sutton)

82. Orange melamine panels were added to cheer the platforms, and escalators were installed to help weary passengers in 1982-83. Sunlight shafts between the two bridges as a Whitechapel-bound train enters on 9th March 1995. (F.Hornby)

83. Mercedes midibuses were small enough to operate through the Rotherhithe Tunnel which is banned to normal size buses. Booking offices along the line remained open for enquiries and the issue of tickets. 1.5m passengers used the station in 1993. (V.Mitchell)

WAPPING

84.   This fine record of the north elevation dates from January 1934. The original building was similar to that at Shoreditch. Few local workers would have appreciated the classical portico when this building was erected in 1915. Hydraulic lifts came into use on 4th October of that year. (L.T.Museum)

85.   The sweeping staircase and tunnel portals were recorded by an artist who depicted quite accurately 2-4-0T no. 98, which was completed at Brighton Works in December 1859. (LUL)

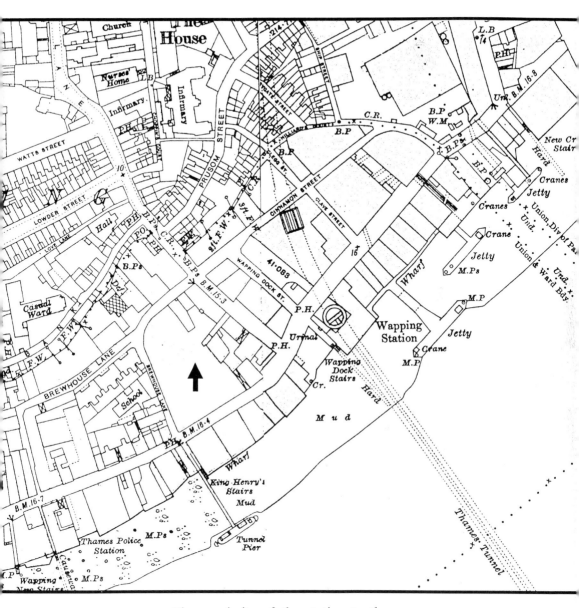

The proximity of the station to the waterfront is evident on this 1914 survey. The cartographer correctly indicates two tunnels.

86. The station was severely damaged during an air raid on 11th September 1940 and a wooden hut had to serve for the next 20 years until rebuilt in brick. One stovepipe is evident. The ventilation/lift shaft is in the background. (H.C.Casserley coll.)

87. The soot-encrusted station had platforms only seven feet wide until 1919 and access was by spiral staircase until 1915. In the 1930s, ladies would request staff to chase away the rats before going on to the platforms. (Lens of Sutton)

88. The foul odour of the tunnel is legendary and staff were issued with air fresheners for use in the trains in the 1980s. Here we witness an ageing Q23 (formerly "G" stock) emerging from the bowels of the earth on 11th September 1971. (R.Palmer)

89. A 1987 view includes the lighting and panelling improvements of a few years earlier, but cables remained exposed. The sound and smell of the river gave this station a unique ambience. Passenger figures dropped from 3.5m in 1873 to 0.9m in 1993. The girders are at the bottom of the lift shaft. (A.C.Mott)

90. A photograph from December 1995 shows some of the cross passages which were a feature of the original design. Work was about to start to reduce the ingress of water through the mud above by means of shotcreting, a system of spraying layers of concrete. (LUL)

91. A 1996 picture features the polygonal rotunda and the 1982 booking office. The tunnel entrance and the surviving staircases down from the lower lift lobby level have Grade II listed status. The body of the Dennis bus was by Wrights of Northern Ireland, hence the unfamiliar registration number. (V.Mitchell)

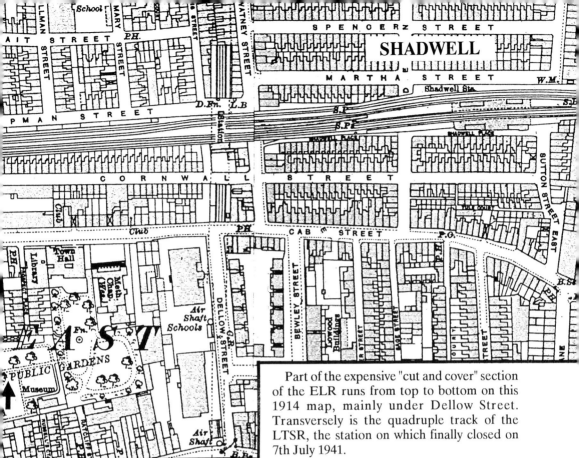

Part of the expensive "cut and cover" section of the ELR runs from top to bottom on this 1914 map, mainly under Dellow Street. Transversely is the quadruple track of the LTSR, the station on which finally closed on 7th July 1941.

92. When photographed in January 1934, the station was in Watney Street and backed onto the ELL. A stairway from the back of the building descended to a landing above the tunnel. From this steps ran down to the platforms and a further flight went up to Chapman Street where doors could still be seen in 1996. A station was opened nearby on the Docklands Light Railway in 1987, the entrance being under the bridge, in its eastern abutment. (L.T.Museum)

93. The damp cavernous interior was photographed in 1986 to show the improvements that would be of greatest benefit to those with tunnel vision. A lift down to a mezzanine floor was added in 1983 and the panels were increased in height in 1996. The arch on the left was once at the foot of the stairs from the building seen in the previous picture. (L.T.Museum)

94. A new entrance was opened in 1983 in Cable Street, a name which records the method of propulsion used on the parallel London & Blackwall Railway in its early years. Much of its route is now used by the DLR, a train on which passes by in this April 1996 photograph. The ELL station was used by 1.3m people in 1993. (V.Mitchell)

FAST ELECTRIC TRAINS FROM THIS STATION TO

MANSION HOUSE	SHADWELL	LIVERPOOL STREET
BLACKFRIARS	WAPPING	FINSBURY PARK
CHARING CROSS	ROTHERHITHE	EUSTON SQUARE
VICTORIA	SURREY DOCKS	KINGS CROSS
WATERLOO	NEW CROSS	PADDINGTON
EARLS COURT		SHEPHERDS BUSH
WALHAM GREEN		HAMMERSMITH

ST MARYS (WHITECHAPEL ROAD) STATION

95. The station was in use from 3rd March 1884 until 1st May 1938. The suffix shown on the sign was added on 26th January 1923. The spur between the ELL and the District Line was used only for football specials, railtours and empty stock movement after 6th October 1941. (L.T.Museum)

WHITECHAPEL

96. The ELR station (right) was the first to open (10th April 1876), the MDR terminus following on 6th October 1884. Trains continued eastwards from 1st February 1902. This photograph is dated 1896. (L.T.Museum)

97. A 1916 view reveals that all activity by then had been concentrated on the ELL premises. The merger took place in 1904. The Brighton service had long ceased but there were still trains to Southend on the DR service from Ealing. (L.T.Museum)

WHITECHAPEL STATION

UNDERGROUND

EAST LONDON, TILBURY, SOUTHEND & DISTRICT RAILWAYS

EVERY FEW MINUTES

TO SURREY DOCKS IN 7 MINUTES

TO NEW CROSS IN 10 MINUTES

EVERY FEW MINUTES

FOR BRIGHTON AND SOUTH COAST

U
FREQUENT TRAINS TO ALL PARTS OF LONDON
. SEE MAP
D

FOR SOUTH EASTERN RAILWAY

CLARA BUTT

98. The ELL platforms are in deep cutting, as this 1952 view towards Shoreditch indicates. Flowerless flower beds remain as a reminder of an attempt to enhance the environment. (R.K.Kirkland)

99. An oil lamp was required on the rear of most electric trains as they would not be impaired by power cuts. A train of 1905 "B" stock was nearing retirement when pictured after arrival from Shoreditch on 23rd August 1952. Note the guard with flag in hand. The girder bridge carries the District Line. (R.K.Kirkland)

100. Class 31 no. D5597 passes on 17th May 1964 with a Chingford to Brighton excursion. The wagons above are in Spitalfields Depot while the rear of the train is close to Whitechapel Sidings junction. (J.J.Smith)

101. The bridge over the ELL was photographed on 10th October 1990 as a Wimbledon-bound train rises up to it. The footbridge links the two island platforms to the booking office. Stairs between these platforms and those of the ELL were added in 1936. (T.Wright)

EAST LONDON RAILWAY.
Available day of issue only.
WAPPING to
WHITECHAPEL(LONDON HOSPITAL)
1d. Third Class 1d.
Issued subject to Regulations in respective Companies' Time Tables.
WHITECHAPEL, L. H.   WHITECHAPEL, L. H.
3764   63764

102. "A60" stock departs for Shoreditch on 21st March 1995 when contractors' cabins were in place in readiness for the refurbishment work on the ELL. (F.Hornby)

103. The work did not involve large quantities of materials and so hand propelled trollies were adequate, as witnessed on 24th April 1996. (V.Mitchell)

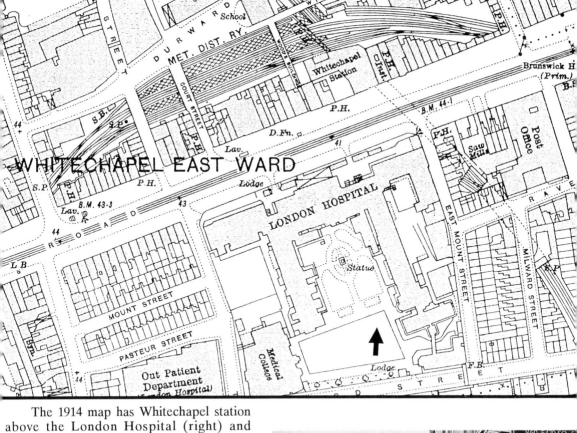

The 1914 map has Whitechapel station above the London Hospital (right) and Whitechapel Junction (between the ELL and St. Mary's Spur) to the right of it. St. Mary's station is opposite St. Mary's Street on the left page.

104. For long the area had a large Jewish community, and excursion posters were produced in Yiddish but the population now has many connections with the Far East. The station is a busy one, handling around 3.7m people in 1993. The canopy was added in the 1930s. (V.Mitchell)

SHOREDITCH

Our journey continues from Whitechapel (lower right) as we pass under Spitalfield Depot and reach the junction for Whitechapel Sidings. These are at a low level and are linked to the former by the hoist marked. This 1914 survey shows the sidings continuing into a tunnel which was intended to form a link with the GER at Cambridge Heath. The GER main line crosses both pages. The ELL passes through two tunnels to reach Shoreditch (top left). Bethnal Green station is top right.

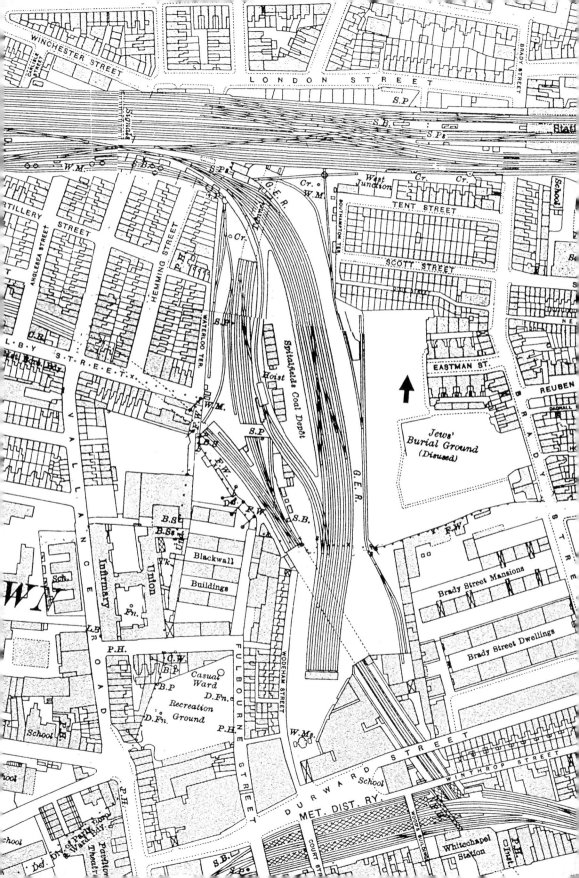

106. A 1952 photograph includes the ends of the conductor rails together with the junction with the former GER lines to Liverpool Street. The connection was severed on 16th April 1966. (R.K.Kirkland)

105. A photograph from May 1901 features LBSCR "Terrier" no. 59 *Cheam*, which was in use from October 1875 until June 1963, except when being rebuilt to class A1X in 1921. Withdrawal of services to Liverpool Street in 1913 was of little consequence to most passengers as the Hammersmith-New Cross trains called at the underground platforms at that station. (R.C.Riley coll.)

107. A sign on the door indicated opening times in 1952. Being a Jewish area, there was a considerable amount of trading on Sunday mornings, notably in the markets in Petticoat Lane and Brick Lane. (R.K.Kirkland)

108. An Eastern to Southern Region excursion passes through the down platform in 1953, as a train of "K" stock waits at the terminal platform. Holden 0-6-0T no. 68613 is in the lead. (J.J.Smith)

109. The Spitalfields hoist could convey two wagons over the 40ft difference in height of the sidings. It has been reported as dating from 1900 but the massive makers nameplate states 1903. In the days before public electric supply, the London Hydraulic Power Company supplied high pressure water for capstans, cranes and lifts. The hoist ceased to be used in November 1955. (J.J.Smith)

110. The street names give the precise location of the entrance. Part of Bishopsgate Goods Depot is in the background. (Lens of Sutton)

111. This eastward view includes the disused down platform, which closed in 1928, and wagons in the high level sidings. The proposed ELL Northern Extension was projected to deviate from the route at the far end of the platforms, but having climbed to a much higher level, approximately that of the wagons top left. (Lens of Sutton)

112. Spitalfields Depot access road is the viewpoint for this panorama which includes pre-fabs on a bomb site, the disused footbridge and a train of "F" stock. The date is 11th March 1956. (J.J.Smith)

113.   The down line was probably removed soon after the connection with BR was severed in April 1966. Stop lamps were first positioned at the near end of the remaining usable platform but later moved to the location shown in this June 1976 photograph. (R.Palmer)

114.   One of London's least known stations, it saw 0.3m passengers in 1993 and was photographed in 1995, little altered since the line opened. (F.Hornby)

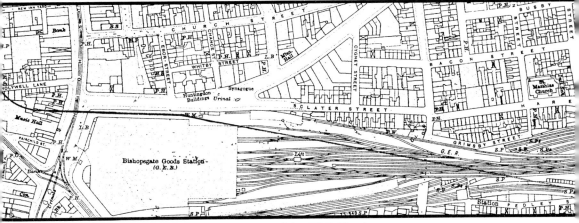

The proposed route of the ELL Northern
Extension has been superimposed on the 1916
map at 15 ins to 1 mile. Shoreditch station is
lower right and the NLR is on the left, the lines
converging from Broad Street lower left.

115.   A photomontage was produced in 1993
to show the predicted appearance of
Shoreditch High Street with the proposed
ELL bridge. This is a southward view.
(LUL/ERM)

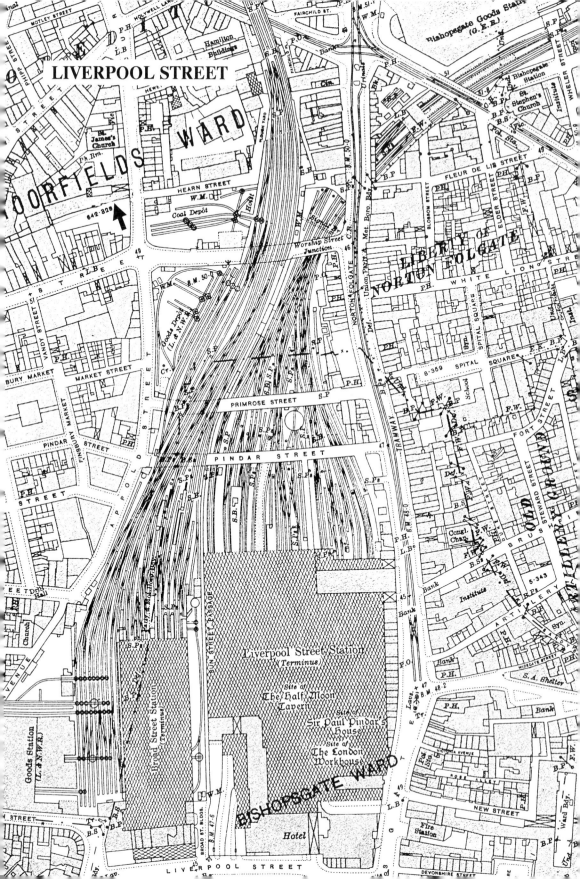

LIVERPOOL STREET

←

In addition to the extensive terminus of the GER, this 20ins to 1 mile survey of 1914 includes that company's Bishopsgate Goods Depot and Bishopsgate Low Level station, the latter being in use until 22nd May 1916.

Services to the NLR's Broad Street terminus slowly withered away in the 1980s. The electric tramway is described in *Aldgate and Stepney Tramways* (Middleton Press).

116. The fine facade of the 1874 station and of the Great Eastern Hotel justified their inclusion on a postcard. The cab road descended steeply from the gate pillars. The fine clock tower was lost during World War II. (Lens of Sutton)

117. Trains for the northern suburbs used the western platforms while local trains for the east occupied the other side, which was completed in 1894. Main line trains had the use of the centre platforms and still have. (Lens of Sutton)

118.   Two main line platforms were longer than the others and were spanned by a foot-bridge. ELL freight services normally reversed at one of the platforms on the eastern side. Platforms 1 & 2 connected with the MR until 1907. Lines shown here continued under the hotel and were used by it for stores until the early 1960s. Regular ELR trains used platform 6 until 1894 when platform 14 was used until 1913. (Lens of Sutton)

119.   Nos. 68575 and 68532 wait to depart under the wires with an Enfield to Hastings excursion on 28th August 1956. There is plenty of steam but no condensing equipment. (A.E.Bennett)

120. Historic stock from the Southern Region (see picture no. 53) stands at platform 18 on 29th March 1958 and serves as a reminder of the variety of trains that have used the ELL over the years. This station was subjected to major alterations between 1988 and 1991 which resulted in this side of the terminus being built over, its loftiness being lost for ever. (R.M.Casserley)

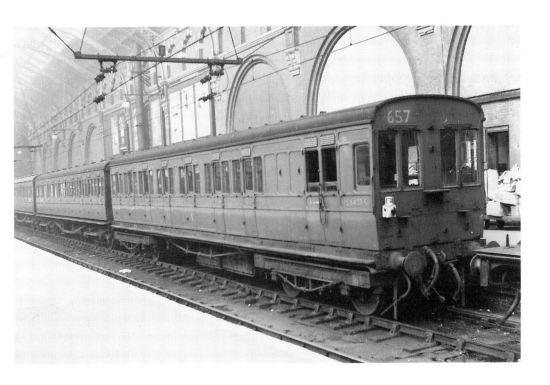

MP Middleton Press

Easebourne Lane, Midhurst. West Sussex. GU29 9AZ   Tel: 01730 813169   Fax: 01730 812601

. . . . . Write or telephone for our latest list . . . . .

BRANCH LINES
Branch Line to Allhallows
Branch Lines to Alton
Branch Lines around Ascot
Branch Line to Bude
Branch Lines around Canterbury
Branch Lines to East Grinstead
Branch Lines around Effingham Jn
Branch Lines to Exmouth
Branch Line to Fairford
Branch Line to Hawkhurst
Branch Lines to Horsham
Branch Line to Ilfracombe
Branch Lines to Longmoor
Branch Line to Lyme Regis
Branch Line to Lynton
Branch Lines around Midhurst
Branch Line to Minehead
Branch Lines to Newport
Branch Line to Padstow
Branch Lines around Portmadoc 1923-46
Branch Lines around Porthmadog 1954-94
Branch Lines to Seaton & Sidmouth
Branch Line to Selsey
Branch Lines around Sheerness
Branch Line to Southwold
Branch Line to Swanage
Branch Line to Tenterden
Branch Lines to Torrington
Branch Lines to Tunbridge Wells
Branch Line to Upwell
Branch Lines around Weymouth

LONDON SUBURBAN RAILWAYS
Caterham and Tattenham Corner
Clapham Jn. to Beckenham Jn.
Crystal Palace and Catford Loop
Holborn Viaduct to Lewisham
Lines aound Wimbledon
London Bridge to Addiscombe
Mitcham Junction Lines
South London Line
West Croydon to Epsom
Willesden Junction to Richmond
Wimbledon to Epsom

STEAMING THROUGH
Steaming through Cornwall
Steaming through East Sussex
Steaming through the Isle of Wight
Steaming through Surrey
Steaming through West Hants
Steaming through West Sussex

GREAT RAILWAY ERAS
Ashford from Steam to Eurostar
Festiniog in the Fifties

COUNTRY BOOKS
Brickmaking in Sussex
East Grinstead Then and Now

SOUTH COAST RAILWAYS
Ashford to Dover
Bournemouth to Weymouth
Brighton to Eastbourne
Brighton to Worthing
Chichester to Portsmouth
Dover to Ramsgate
Hastings to Ashford
Ryde to Ventnor
Worthing to Chichester

SOUTHERN MAIN LINES
Bromley South to Rochester
Charing Cross to Orpington
Crawley to Littlehampton
Dartford to Sittingbourne
East Croydon to Three Bridges
Epsom to Horsham
Exeter to Barnstaple
Exeter to Tavistock
Faversham to Dover
Haywards Heath to Seaford
London Bridge to East Croydon
Orpington to Tonbridge
Sittingbourne to Ramsgate
Swanley to Ashford
Tonbridge to Hastings
Victoria to Bromley South
Waterloo to Windsor
Woking to Portsmouth
Woking to Southampton
Yeovil to Exeter

COUNTRY RAILWAY ROUTES
Andover to Southampton
Bath to Evercreech Junction
Bournemouth to Evercreech Jn
Burnham to Evercreech Junction
Croydon to East Grinstead
East Kent Light Railway
Fareham to Salisbury
Frome to Bristol
Guildford to Redhill
Porthmadog to Blaenau
Reading to Basingstoke
Reading to Guildford
Redhill to Ashford
Salisbury to Westbury
Strood to Paddock Wood
Taunton to Barnstaple
Westbury to Bath
Woking to Alton

TROLLEYBUS CLASSICS
Croydon's Trolleybuses
Woolwich & Dartford Trolleybuses

TRAMWAY CLASSIC
Aldgate & Stepney Tramways
Bournemouth & Poole Tramways
Brighton's Tramways
Bristol's Tramways
Camberwell & W. Norwood Tramw
Croydon's Tramways
Dover's Tramways
East Ham & West Ham Tramway
Eltham & Woolwich Tramways
Embankment & Waterloo Tramwa
Exeter & Taunton Tramways
Greenwich & Dartford Tramways
Hampstead & Highgate Tramway
Hastings Tramways
Holborn & Finsbury Tramways
Ilford & Barking Tramways
Kingston & Wimbledon Tramways
Lewisham & Catford Tramways
Maidstone & Chatham Tramways
North Kent Tramways
Portsmouth's Tramways
Seaton & Eastbourne Tramways
Southampton Tramways
Southend-on-sea Tramways
Thanet's Tramways
Victoria & Lambeth Tramways
Walthamstow & Leyton Tramways
Wandsworth & Battersea Tramway

OTHER RAILWAY BOOKS
Garraway Father & Son
Industrial Railways of the South Eas
London Chatham & Dover Railwa
South Eastern Railway
War on the Line

MILITARY BOOKS
Battle over Portsmouth
Battle Over Sussex 1940
Blitz Over Sussex 1941-42
Bognor at War
Bombers over Sussex 1943-45
Military Defence of West Sussex

WATERWAY ALBUMS
Hampshire Waterways
Kent and East Sussex Waterways
London to Portsmouth Waterway
West Sussex Waterways

BUS BOOK
Eastbourne Bus Story

SOUTHERN RAILWAY ● VIDEOS ●
Memories of the Hayling Island Branc
Memories of the Lyme Regis Branch
War on the Line